IMAGES
of Sport

BRISTOL CITY
FOOTBALL CLUB
1966-2002

Bolton Wanderers *v.* Bristol City 1985/86. The front cover of the programme for City's first ever visit to Wembley. Bolton were beaten 3-0 in the Freight Rover Final on 24 May in front of a 54,502-strong crowd. The encounter generated receipts of £286,281.

IMAGES
of Sport

BRISTOL CITY
FOOTBALL CLUB
1966-2002

Tom Hopegood and David Woods

TEMPUS

Dedication

In memory of two staunch City supporters, John Charles Hopegood (1931-2001) and Edward David Woods (1917-1969).

First published 2002, reprinted 2003

Tempus Publishing Limited
The Mill, Brimscombe Port,
Stroud, Gloucestershire, GL5 2QG

British Library Cataloguing in Publication Data.
A catalogue record for this book is available from the British Library.

ISBN 0 7524 2417 3

Typesetting and origination by Tempus Publishing Limited
Printed in Great Britain by Midway Colour Print, Wiltshire

Contents

Foreword

I watched City from the terraces in the early 1960s, when my hero was Bobby (Shadow) Williams. The forward line in those days had skill in abundance and readily scored goals, especially in the 1962/63 campaign, when all five front men (Alex Tait 10, John Atyeo 16, Brian Clark 23, Bobby Williams 19, and Jantzen Derrick 10) reached double figures as City raced to the century mark.

Spotted by ex-City captain Cliff Morgan, I joined the club in the summer of 1968 and played for the reserves whilst still at school. I was captain of the youth team of 1969/70, which reached the semi-final of the FA Youth Cup, of whom five members, Ray Cashley, Gerry Gow, Tom Ritchie, Dave Rodgers and myself, went on to play in the top flight.

With the side struggling following the transfer of Bobby Kellard to Leicester to help pay for the Dolman Stand, Alan Dicks gave me my first-team debut at Middlesbrough in October 1970. Fortunately, the acquisition on loan of Brian Hill and Les Wilson helped steer the club to safety and the following season, despite the sale of Chris Garland to Chelsea, brought a vast improvement thanks to the capture of Gerry Sweeney from Greenock Morton and John Emanuel from Ferndale.

I played as a regular in 1972/73 when the promotion side was very much beginning to take shape. The cup run of 1973/74 was one of the highlights of my career, and I was in the team throughout, despite not always seeing eye to eye with Alan Dicks! My goal in the fifth round against Leeds at Ashton Gate is fondly remembered, as is the pass I laid on for Donnie Gillies to fire in the Elland Road winner.

By 1975 City were a good Second Division side with Paul Cheesley a class act at centre forward. A fine blend of local lads and Scots gave City the chance to take on the best, but Cheesley's career-ending injury upset the balance. After a tense struggle, our newly-won status was retained, but the following year I moved on to Plymouth, where a certain Malcolm Allison made sure that life was never dull.

Keith Fear

Introduction

As 1966 is a defining moment in British football, with Alf Ramsay's wingless wonders winning the World Cup, it seemed sensible to overlap slightly with the first Bristol City volume and to commence this book from that time, given that Alan Dicks, who took over as manager from Fred Ford, was one of the most slavish adherents of a doctrine that was to produce so many negative tacticians.

The season leading up to the World Cup had seen the City almost gain promotion to the top flight, and their finishing position of fifth had the fans ever hopeful of the prize being obtained in 1966/67, despite John Atyeo's retirement. Unfortunately they were out of sorts right from the off, but by the end of the campaign the team had been reinvigorated by the capture of Johnny Quigley, Chris Crowe and Hugh McIlmoyle. Expectations were high at the start of 1967/68, but again they struggled and it wasn't long before Fred Ford was dismissed and Coventry's assistant manager Alan Dicks was appointed in his place.

From then on it was downhill all the way as far as entertainment was concerned, although to be fair the new man did save City from relegation. It was the capture of ace scorer John Galley from Rotherham United that turned things round, although he was greatly helped by the inspired play of Johnny Quigley. Galley was not the most elegant of footballers, and he was certainly not as skilful as the man he replaced, Hugh McIlmoyle; but he had no equal in scoring goals, even if they did fly in off all parts of his person.

Surprisingly, Dicks let the creative Quigley go in the close season of 1968, and replaced him, for a record £36,000 fee, with the nomadic Bobby Kellard. The new man, a real pocket-battleship in midfield, did much to steady things as City began to acquire a reputation for rough play. The summer of 1970 saw the Dolman Stand being built, but the cost of the project necessitated the sale of all the club houses, as well as the departure of Kellard to Leicester. Another relegation battle ensued, and the inspired loan signings of Brian Hill and Les Wilson were required to haul the club to safety. Indeed, the season's only highlight was City's progress to the semi-finals of the Football League Cup.

Chairman Harry Dolman demanded an improvement in 1971/72, and he got it as new replaced old. A half dozen of the team that started the season were destined to be part of City's promotion squad four years hence. By dint of work rate, rather than spectacular displays, they became a respected Second Division side.

One of the greatest shocks in the history of the FA Cup probably kept Dicks his job in 1973/74 as City won a fifth round replay at Elland Road over the side destined to be that season's League Champions. Two years later, the club reaped the benefit as a place in the top-flight was regained after 65 long years of waiting. The omens were good as City performed brilliantly in an opening day win at Highbury, but despite the capture of Norman Hunter from Leeds in the autumn, it took a draw in their last match at Coventry to prevent a quick return to the lower division.

Sadly this stay of execution did not last long, even though it did look for a while in 1978/79 as if City were becoming established among the elite. Unfortunately, the departure of the inspirational Hunter in the summer heralded a disastrous 1979/80 campaign that ended in relegation.

If this wasn't bad enough, even worse was to follow as City's decline continued. With the team struggling in the Second Division, Dicks was replaced by Bob Houghton, the man who had taken Swedish club Malmo to the European Cup Final in 1979. Unfortunately, Houghton was unable to arrest the slump and with the introduction of three points for a win for 1981/82, City's whole defensive credo was in tatters.

As City slid out of the Second Division and tumbled into the lower reaches of the Third, the only bright spot was the capture of centre-forward Mick Harford at the start of the 1981/82 campaign. Unfortunately, while Harford was undoubtedly a great player, even he wasn't able to save City as the financial crisis, which had been hovering around for a few years, erupted. Houghton resigned at the turn of the year and the club went into receivership before being restructured as Bristol City 1982 PLC. Players were sold off and, having to make do with many youngsters in the side, relegation to the Fourth became inevitable long before the end of season.

The new organisation appointed ex-Rovers boss Terry Cooper as player/manager and slowly the City began to improve, though not before sinking right to the bottom of the whole Football League in December 1982. From now on, the only way was up, and the following season City secured promotion by winning their last game 2-1 at Chester.

Whilst the football was always exciting under Cooper's charge, consistency was a scarce commodity. The Freight Rovers Trophy was won on City's first ever visit to Wembley in 1985/86, but the following season's failure in a penalty shoot-out at the same stadium cost them the chance of a great double. Joe Jordan took over in March 1988, and he was to take City to their second appearance in the semi-finals of the Football League Cup, before gaining the promotion prize in 1989/90, when they were pipped to the Championship by Bristol Rovers.

Jordan's departure to Heart of Midlothian in September 1990 precipitated a disastrous decade for the club, with boardroom unrest being reflected by many poor performances on the pitch. Jimmy Lumsden took over, but was soon replaced by Denis Smith, who turned City around at the end of 1991/92 by playing some vintage football following the signings of Leroy Rosenior and Andy Cole. Player-power seemed to be behind the poor form of 1992/93 which led to Smith's departure and the appointment of Russell Osman. The new man saved City from relegation, but at a cost: City's dour football the following campaign saw gates tumble, despite a magnificent win at Anfield in the FA Cup. Performances were dire at the start of 1994/95, and despite the return of Joe Jordan to the hot-seat, things hardly improved, and City found themselves relegated for the ninth time in their history.

To many fans, this spoke volumes about the Reform Group board, who had come to power on the back of many statements of intent, one such objective being Premiership status within five years. Fortunately Scott Davidson put another board together to kick-start City once more. With Scott displaying much vigour, everything looked promising when, following the appointment of John Ward as manager, City gained promotion in 1997/98. Unfortunately history tells that nothing stays rosy in the City's garden for long, so it should have come as no surprise when it all went wrong the following year, with the Club once again displaying its propensity to shoot itself in the proverbial foot.

With Davidson taking on the paid role of chief executive, and former manager Russell Osman having returned to the club in a backroom job, the stage wasn't best set for the season, despite the fact that a record amount of money had been found to purchase some talented players. A poor start had City struggling, but a great 2-1 home win over Bolton suggested that a corner had been turned. Unfortunately, the bombshell broke the following day with the departure of Ward and the appointment Swedish coach Benny Lannartsson. The club was in turmoil, and relegation was the outcome. Lannartsson was replaced by Tony Pulis for the start of 1999/2000, whilst Davidson was replaced as chairman by John Laycock. The style of the new man's football didn't go down well with City fans however, and it was a relief to most of them when Pulis left to join Portsmouth after less than six months in charge. He was replaced by Tony Fawthrop, who in turn gave way to the present incumbent Danny Wilson at the start of 2000/01.

Surprisingly the fans have remained loyal, with record season ticket sales for the past five seasons – but many feel it is now time for the club to reward such dedication by producing their first Championship winning side in almost 50 years.

Note:
Most of the attendance figures, and receipts, contained in this book are as recorded by the Football League and as such can differ from information in the newspapers. Unless otherwise stated the matches referred to in this work are League games.

One
World Cup Hangover

Tactics talk by Fred Ford 1966/67. City boss Fred Ford (extreme right) briefs his forward line prior to City's 4-1 FA Cup replay win over Fourth Division Halifax Town in front of a 23,188 crowd on 31 January. From left to right: Johnny Quigley, Jantzen Derrick, Terry Bush, Chris Crowe, Roger Peters.

Bristol City pre-season training, 1966. City get down to pre-season training on the Bristol Oil & Cake Mills ground on the Portway.

Bristol City Youth. City's flourishing youth policy is illustrated by this group of Ashton Gate youngsters. From left to right, back row: Stephen Morris, Robert Williams, John Macey, Graham Tanner, David Jenkins, Trevor Tainton. Front row: John Munday, Chris Garland, David Down, John Giles, Danny Bartley. (Interestingly, Macey, Tainton, Garland, Down, Giles and Bartley all made their mark at Ashton Gate.)

Above: Harry Dolman. The longest-serving Bristol City chairman, who had almost twenty-five years at the helm (from 23 March 1949 until 13 March 1974, when he became club president), is pictured here on the left handing over benefit cheques to City greats Bobby Etheridge and John Atyeo. Born on 6 August 1897, Dolman joined the Board in 1938 and died on 9 November 1977.

Right: John Atyeo, King Of Goals. The cover of Atyeo's testimonial brochure shows him coming onto the pitch for his last League game, which was won 4-1 against Ipswich Town in front of 13,893 spectators at Ashton Gate on 10 May 1966. Atyeo notched two goals in this match, to take his total to what was thought at the time to be 350 in League and Cup appearances for the City, though subsequent research suggests the figure may have actually been 349.

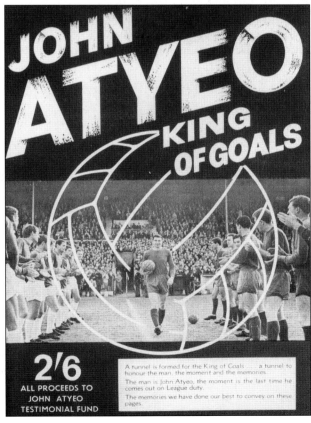

JOHN ATYEO KING OF GOALS

2/6
ALL PROCEEDS TO JOHN ATYEO TESTIMONIAL FUND

A tunnel is formed for the King of Goals . . . a tunnel to honour the man, the moment and the memories.

The man is John Atyeo, the moment is the last time he comes out on League duty.

The memories we have done our best to convey on these pages.

Bristol City *v*. Leeds United, 1966/67. Receipts of £3,930 came from the 17,425 crowd who saw Atyeo bring the curtain down on his soccer career in this his testimonial, which City lost 4-2 on 10 October. Unfortunately they were not rewarded with a goal from the great man, although they did see Atyeo and Jack Charlton parade the World Cup around the Ashton Gate pitch during half time. *Left:* Atyeo is cheered on to the pitch. *Right:* Atyeo in action during the game.

The Young Robins' shop, 1967/68. The Programme & Souvenir Shop opened at the start of the season and this picture, which appeared in the programme for the Queens Park Rangers game – which City lost 2-0 on 22 August – shows Mrs Margaret Bidgood and Mrs Shirley Pearson arranging the many books, emblems, souvenirs and programmes on sale to supporters young and old.

Bristol Casuals, 1966/67. With the advent of local Sunday League Football, a group of City supporters formed this club at the King's Head, Bedminster Down, on 14 July 1966, whilst their Rovers counterparts across the river started up the Pirates. The Bristol & District Amateur Sunday Football League commenced operations on 4 September 1966 with a programme of twelve matches, among which was a 9-5 defeat for the Casuals against the Showmen's Guild on Clevedon Town's old ground at Teignmouth Road.

Fortunately it didn't take the Casuals long to chalk up their first win, as the following week, when the above photograph was taken, the South Western Regional Hospital Board were beaten 4-2 in front of 60 spectators at Brentry Hospital. From left to right, back row: Pete Lomas (captain), Dave Lea, Bob Sage, Mike Hann, Alan Davey, Jerry Comerford. Front row: Norman Bishop (treasurer), Dave Crooks, Bob Powell, Dave Woods (secretary), Dave Hunt. The club's record victory was a 13-3 home success over Ranella Rangers in a Second Division game at Manor Road, Keynsham on 20 October 1968.

Right: Bristol & District Amateur Sunday Football League Cup final, 1966/67 – the programme for what was only the second Sunday League Cup Final played on a Football League ground. Just five weeks after suffering a shock 2-1 home defeat at the hands of the lowly Casuals, the Backwell side came good at Ashton Gate with a 4-0 victory over Brislington Combination on 7 May in front of a crowd of 3,000.

BRISTOL & DISTRICT AMATEUR SUNDAY FOOTBALL LEAGUE
(AFFILIATED TO THE GLOUCESTERSHIRE COUNTY F.A.)

President: Robin Perry, Esq.   Vice President: Ray Wood, Esq.

Chairman: League Secretary: Treasurer:
S. T. RUMMINS   R. SAUNDERS   M. B. THOMAS

League Management Committee:
F. Bond, D. Hughes, C. Strong, B. Langley, J. Bennett.

SUNDAY CUP FINAL
AT ASHTON GATE, BRISTOL

Backwell Sunday

v.

Brislington Combination

Sunday, May 7th, 1967

(With kind permission of Bristol City F.C.)

Kick-off 3.15 p.m.   Programme 1/6

DYER PRINTING CO.

Letterpress and Lithographic Printers Paper Merchants and Stationers

96–98 WEST STREET, BEDMINSTER, BRISTOL 3

Telephone 661426

Bristol City programmes, 1966/67 and 1967/68. *Left:* This issue for the opening home game against Crystal Palace, which was lost 1-0 in front of 13,365 fans, was the journal's first re-vamp in ten seasons. *Right:* The commencement of the 1967/68 campaign brought a change in the design of the front cover with this issue for the match against Huddersfield Town on 19 August. Inside, however, the content for the 16-page issue was similar to that of the previous campaign, as was the result of the game, as City went down to another defeat – this time, however, by a more exciting 3-2 scoreline in front of 18,148 spectators.

Bristol City 1967/68. The City first-team squad that commenced the season with Fred Ford in charge. Left to right, back row: Fred Ford (manager), Jack Connor, Gordon Parr, Alec Briggs, Mike Gibson, Gordon Low, Terry Bush, Tony Ford, Les Bardsley (physiotherapist). Middle row: Chuck Drury, Jantzen Derrick, Chris Crowe, Hugh McIlmoyle, Johnny Quigley, Roger 'Lou' Peters. Front row: Ray Savino, Gerry Sharpe, Danny Bartley.

Ipswich Town *v*. Bristol City, 1967/68. City conceded a 5-0 defeat in this Second Division game in front of a 13,702 crowd at Portman Road on 26 August. In this picture, which appeared in the *Soccer Star* of 15 September, the Ipswich 'keeper Ken Hancock clutches the ball to prevent City's Chris Crowe (second from the left) from scoring. This was City's third successive loss since the start of the season.

Bristol City *v*. Blackpool, 1967/68. City's 'Lou' Peters challenges Blackpool 'keeper Alan Taylor for the ball during the 4-2 home defeat in front of a 13,191 crowd. The match, which brought in gate receipts of £2,464.19.0, was played on 16 September. This defeat, played in front of the 'Match of the Day' cameras, left City at the bottom of the Second Division table, and brought an end to Fred Ford's reign.

City's captain Gordon Low (right) is pictured with Bristol Rovers pair Bernard Hall (centre) and Alfie Biggs during the photo shoot for Hall's testimonial brochure in 1967/68. Low was much underrated by many City fans, but he was a fine midfielder who gave good service after signing from Huddersfield Town for £3,000 in March 1961. Unfortunately, with the coming of Alan Dicks, this Aberdeen-born player fell out of favour. He moved on to Stockport County in July 1968 for a fee of £3,000, before ending his League career with a brief spell at Crewe Alexandra.

Bristol City and Rovers, 1967/68. This photograph of fraternising City and Rovers players appeared in the centre pages of Bernard Hall's testimonial brochure. Rovers 'keeper Hall had his career cut short following a collision with Middlesbrough's John O'Rourke early in the second half of the League meeting at Eastville on New Year's Eve 1966. Unconscious for sixteen days, Hall demonstrated all his renowned courage in battling back from his serious head injuries, but his soccer career was finished at the early age of twenty-five. A crowd of almost 9,000 attended his benefit game on 16 October 1967, when a Combined Bristol XI lost 4-3 against West Ham United.

Above left: John Quigley, City's most skilful midfielder of the 1960s, came to Ashton Gate in November 1966 from Huddersfield Town in a swap deal involving Brian Clark. An FA Cup winner with Nottingham Forest in 1958/59, it was a surprise to many when Dicks sold him to Mansfield for just £3,000 at the end of the 1967/68 season.

Above right: Chris Crowe, a signing from Wolverhampton Wanderers and an England international, electrified the City side in the second half of the 1966/67 season. Unfortunately he rarely reproduced such form thereafter and was transferred to Australian club Auburn during the 1968/69 season.

Right: A man with a mission, 1967/68. Alan Dicks was appointed as City manager in succession to the popular Fred Ford on 5 October 1967. A player with Chelsea and Southend United, he was part of the Sky Blue revolution at Coventry as assistant to that great innovator Jimmy Hill. This article appeared in the programme for the home meeting with Cardiff, which was drawn 1-1 in front of 15,609 fans, producing receipts of £3,083.7.0 on 14 October 1967.

Alan Dicks — a man with a mission

Alan Dicks was appointed Bristol City's new manager at a special meeting of directors on Thursday, October 5. We feel sure we have made an excellent appointment and we trust that everyone with the interests of Bristol City at heart will pull with him rather than against him.

He was born in London 31 years ago and played first of all for Chelsea at wing-half or centre-half. Later he moved to Southend United before becoming assistant manager at Coventry City in January 1962.

At Coventry he was directly involved in the re-organisation and ultimate success of Coventry reaching the First Division this season.

Last Saturday Coventry generously released him to watch our team play at Crystal Palace. And this week both manager Jimmy Hill and chairman Derrick Robins have allowed him as much time as possible to concentrate on the affairs and needs of Bristol City.

We have always had a close relationship with Coventry and we should like to thank them again for allowing Mr. Dicks to spend so much time in Bristol this week.

Alan is married with five children and he and his wife have been looking at houses in Bristol this week. They are as anxious to get settled in Bristol as we are to have Mr. Dicks working full-time for the

17

CHRIS SCORES

Our last goal—Chris Crowe's header against Cardiff City. The massed Cardiff defence is powerless as Chris falls after heading our equaliser in the last home match.

Below: Roger Peters is spectacularly tackled by Cardiff fullback Bobby Ferguson in the same match.

Left: Bristol City *v.* Cardiff City 1967/68. In front of a 15,609 Ashton Gate crowd, Chris Crowe heads in City's 57th minute equaliser on 14 October. This draw was sufficient to take City off the foot of the table.

Below: Ken Wimshurst. The new manager's first signing at a fee of £12,000 was this midfielder from Southampton. A cult figure at the Dell, he was a mainstay in the City team for four years before joining the Ashton Gate coaching staff. He subsequently had a spell as caretaker manager between the departure of Alan Dicks in 1980 and the arrival of Bob Houghton. Previously he had been on the books of Newcastle United, Gateshead and Wolverhampton Wanderers.

Left: John Galley's debut, 1967/68. Signed from Rotherham United, a leg injury prevented Galley from making his City debut until mid-December at Huddersfield. It was worth the wait though, as he scored all City's goals in a great 3-0 win at Leeds Road, as was reported on the front page of the *Bristol Evening Post Green'Un* of 16 December 1967.

Bristol City *v.* Ipswich Town, 1967/68. John Galley (fifth from the left) beats goalkeeper Ken Hancock with a header into the top corner of the net. It looked a fine effort, but the referee disallowed the goal, which would have doubled City's advantage. At the finish, they had to settle for a 1-1 draw in this game played in front of 17,628 fans, who paid receipts of £3,816.6.6 on 22 December.

Middlesbrough *v.* Bristol City, 1967/68. Agony for Gordon Parr at Ayresome Park in the 4th round of the FA Cup on 17 February. In this *Soccer Star* illustration, he catches Mike Gibson unawares with his attempted back-pass to give Middlesbrough an eighth minute lead. Fortunately, City fought back well to earn a creditable 1-1 draw in front of 29,086 fans who generated receipts of £7,913.9.6. In the Ashton Gate replay three days later, a 21,771 crowd (£5,743.10.0) saw City win 2-1 to progress through to the next round.

And the dog ran away

with the ball !

Left: Hull City *v.* Bristol City 1967/68. An amusing interlude during City's 4-2 defeat in front of 12,596 fans at Boothferry Park on 10 February. As Mike Gibson was about to take a goal-kick the intervention of a dog delayed proceedings for some five minutes.

Above right: Terry Bush. City's never-say-die hero was a tremendous servant at Ashton Gate, and never gave less than his best. Possessor of a terrific cannonball shot, he burst onto the first-team scene with a great first-minute goal on his debut on 31 March 1961 when City drew 2-2 with Torquay United. Unfortunately his career was cut short by knee problems, and he became City's assistant secretary before working for the Transport and General Workers Union.

Bristol City, 1967/68. The City first-team squad under their new manager, Alan Dicks. From left to right, back row: Gordon Parr, Terry Bush, Jack Connor, Tony Ford, Mike Gibson, Alec Briggs, Chris Garland, Ken Wimshurst, Les Bardsley (physiotherapist). Front row: Danny Bartley, Jantzen Derrick, Chris Crowe, Alan Dicks (manager), John Galley, Johnny Quigley, Roger 'Lou' Peters, Trevor Jacobs.

THE LAST TIME—Elland Road, March 9th, 1968.
Top: **GERRY SHARPE** heads for goal as **JOHN QUIGLEY** moves in front of **JACK CHARLTON**.
Left: **KEN WIMSHURST** and **JOHNNY GILES** in action.
Above: **JOHN QUIGLEY** gets in a centre as **PETER LORIMER** challenges.
Evening Post pictures by **JACK GARLAND**.

Leeds United *v*. Bristol City, 1967/68. Action from the hot-tempered FA Cup fifth round clash at Elland Road which City lost 2-0 on 9 March in front of a 45,227 crowd who paid £15,250 receipts. In this game the Leeds 'keeper Gary Sprake was sent off in the 72nd minute for punching Chris Garland.

JOHN GETS UP TO IT

Left: Bristol City *v.* Portsmouth 1967/68. Pompey 'keeper John Milkins fails to gather Lou Peters' corner and John Galley leaps above Ron Tindall to head in the 84th minute goal that seals City's 3-0 win on 16 March in front of a 16,065 (£3,159.9.0) spectators at Ashton Gate. *Above:* Chris Garland, City's golden boy, was an England Under-21 international who transferred to Chelsea for £110,000 early in the 1971/72 campaign. He subsequently played for Leicester City before returning to Ashton Gate in 1976/77, when his goals helped to save City from relegation.

The Dolman Stand, 1968/69. Following the demolition of the No Two Stand, affectionately referred to as the Cow Shed, during the summer of 1966, this model by E.S. & A. Robinson Architects was revealed as its proposed replacement in 1968. Work on this new stand, which was named after City's chairman, commenced during January 1969 and was ready for the start of the 1970/71 season.

Mike Gibson impressed in his performances for Shrewsbury against the City, and it was a fortunate day when this courageous 'keeper moved to Ashton Gate towards the end of the 1962/63 campaign. Undoubtedly the best 'keeper the club has had since the war, he did much to help City retain their Second Division status during the late 1960s. He moved to Gillingham in July 1972 and appeared in 80 League games for them before retiring at the end of the 1973/74 campaign.

Above: Fulham *v.* Bristol City, 1968/69. City commenced the season at Craven Cottage against newly relegated Fulham. Unfortunately Johnny Haynes, who is shown on the left of this picture holding off Ken Wimshurst's challenge, inspired the Cottagers to a 1-0 win in front of 16,572 supporters on 10 August.

Left: Jantzen Derrick was one of the most skilful players to have graced the Ashton Gate scene. This photograph appeared in the City programme for the game versus Cardiff on 23 August 1969. After starring in the English Schoolboys side, Derrick was City's youngest player when he made his debut in a 3-1 defeat at Lincoln on 28 November 1959. Although he was trailed by the likes of West Ham, he remained at Ashton Gate until going on loan to Mansfield in March 1971 and then having a spell with Paris St-Germain.

Gerry Sharpe, one of City's brightest stars, had his exciting career cut short by a broken leg sustained during the 2-0 home defeat by Middlesbrough on 16 January 1971. Gloucester-born, he made his debut during the promotion campaign of 1964/65 when he proved adept at scoring in away matches.

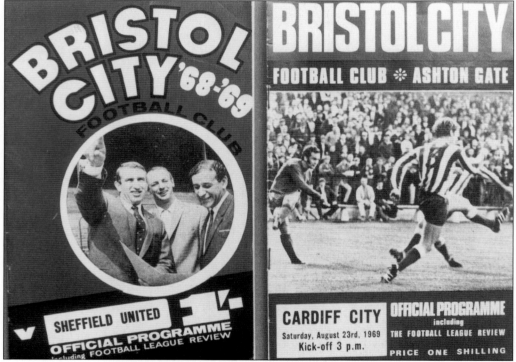

Bristol City programmes, 1968/69 and 1969/70. *Left:* Although the basic programme remained at 16 pages in 1968/69, it was produced on better quality paper and had the *Football League Review* stapled inside. The cover design was such that a different picture was able to be shown for each match, as shown by this issue for City's opening home League game against Sheffield United on 17 August, which was drawn 1-1 in front of a 19,280 crowd, who paid receipts of £4,157.18.0. *Right:* For the following season, the cover design was changed, but again a different picture was featured on the front of every issue. This game against Cardiff City on 23 August was lost 2-0.

Blackburn Rovers v. Bristol City 1968/69. John Galley scores in City's 3-1 win in front of a 7,566 crowd at Ewood Park on 22 March.

One in, one out for Gerry

GERRY SHARPE and JOHN GALLEY climb together to meet BOBBY KELLARD'S centre against Exeter. Sharpe got there first and netted his first goal of the season.

Almost another goal for GERRY. He slips the ball just wide of the post with Exeter player-manager JOHNNY NEWMAN powerless to intervene. Pictures: John Cottle.

Bristol City v. Exeter City 1969/70. *Top:* Gerry Sharpe, whose career was destined to be so cruelly ended by injury 17 months later, heads in City's third goal in the 69th minute of their 3-2 League Cup replay success in front of a 10,924 Ashton Gate crowd on 19 August. *Bottom:* Further action from the Exeter game shows Sharpe slipping the ball wide of the post, with Exeter player-boss Johnny Newman powerless to intervene.

Above: Bristol City *v*. Queens Park Rangers 1969/70. Centre-half Dickie Rooks (third from the right), moves up to try a shot during City's 2-0 win in front of a 18,893 (£3,991.16.0) Ashton Gate crowd on 15 November.

Left: Bobby Kellard. City's dynamic midfield general, cost the club a record £36,300 when he was signed from Portsmouth, but they in turn received a record £49,000 from Leicester when he moved on in the close season of 1971.

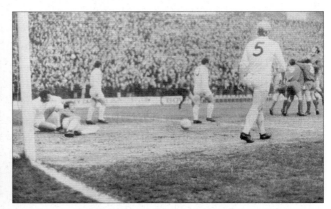

Above: Charlton Athletic *v*. Bristol City 1969/70. City went down to a 2-1 defeat against relegation-threatened Charlton in front of a 15,972 crowd at the Valley on 14 April. This picture, from the June 1970 issue of *Charles Buchan's Football Monthly*, shows the dejected City players (in white), from left to right: Gordon Parr, Mike Gibson, Trevor Jacobs, Bobby Kellard and Dickie Rooks, trooping back to the centre circle, whilst Charlton's Alan Campbell is mobbed by his jubilant team-mates after popping in the 13th minute opening goal.

Two
Progress

Bristol City line-up, 1970/71. From left to right, back row: Trevor Jacobs, Jantzen Derrick, Alan Skirton, Gordon Parr, Mike Gibson, Jack Connor, John Galley, Chris Garland, Ken Wimshurst. Front row: Danny Bartley, Trevor Tainton, Gerry Sharpe, Dickie Rooks (captain), Brian Drysdale, Geoff Merrick, Gerry Gow.

Bristol City *v*. West Ham United, 1970/71. In front of a 9,655 crowd for this pre-season friendly against West Ham United on 5 August, Chris Garland hammers in City's winner.

Charlton Athletic *v*. Bristol City, 1970/71. Chris Garland, in white, fires wide at the Valley during City's 1-1 draw in front of a 10,460 crowd on 22 August.

Above: Bristol City *v.* Cardiff City, 1970/71. Gerry Sharpe ends the Welsh bogey as in front of a 24,969 (£6,382.3.0) Ashton Gate crowd on 29 August he nets the only goal of the game in the 89th minute, securing City's first home Severnside derby win since April 1958.

Right: Green 'Un, 1970/71. How the *Green' Un* of 29 August reported City's win over Cardiff.

Above: Bristol City Reserves *v.* Fulham Reserves, 1970/71. In front of a 1,567 crowd David Bruton heads clear watched by team-mate Billy Menmuir in a 3-0 Football Combination win at Ashton Gate on 19 September.

BLACKBURN
Saturday September 26
Kick-off 3 p.m.

OFFICIAL PROGRAMME
including
THE FOOTBALL LEAGUE REVIEW

PRICE ONE SHILLING

Above right: Bristol City *v.* Blackburn Rovers 1970/71. The front cover of this programme is unusual in that it actually depicts reserve team action from the game against Fulham on 19 September. David Rodgers (left) is shown sliding into the tackle as goals from Keith Fear, Billy Menmuir and Trevor Jacobs allowed the Reserves to maintain their unbeaten record.

A drop of the hard stuff . . . .

Manager of the Month, 1970/71. City boss Alan Dicks (left) receives his Bell's Division Two Manager of the Month award for August from David Lloyd at the home game against Hull City, which was drawn 3-3 in front of a 12,978 (£2,701.13.6) crowd on 12 September.

Bristol City *v*. Blackburn Rovers, 1970/71. Mike Gibson in typical action as he endeavours to keep Blackburn at bay during the 1-1 home draw in front of a 14,019 (£2,891.4.6) crowd on 26 September. The other City players in the picture are Brian Drysdale (left) and Dickie Rooks (centre).

Swindon Town *v*. Bristol City, 1970/71. Mike Gibson foils Swindon star Don Rogers during City's 2-1 defeat on 7 November in front of a 16,678 County Ground crowd.

Bristol City *v*. Fulham, 1970/71. In front of a 23,230 (£8,786.15.0) crowd on 24 November, Gerry Sharpe fires in City's 31st minute penalty winner in the quarter-final replay of the Football League Cup.

Bristol City *v*. Fulham, 1970/71. Further action from the Football League Cup clash with Fulham on 24 November. This photograph shows City's Dickie Rooks (number 5) keeping the visitors at bay during the second half.

Above: Bristol City *v.* Tottenham Hotspur, 1970/71. Action from the Football League Cup semi-final, first leg at Ashton Gate. These two pictures depict the Spurs equaliser in a 1-1 draw in front of 30,201 fans, who paid £13,931.13.0 receipts, on 16 December. Top: Alan Gilzean heading for goal. Bottom. Martin Chivers retrieves the ball after Mike Gibson has been beaten. It took City seven games to reach this stage of the competition, as away draws at Rotherham United (0-0), Leicester City (2-2) and Fulham (0-0) meant replays before these sides were respectively disposed of 4-0, 2-1 (a.e.t.) and 1-0. Only First Division Blackpool succumbed at the first time of asking, defeated 1-0 in the third round at Bloomfield Road on 7 October.

Right: Tottenham Hotspur *v.* Bristol City, 1970/71. The front cover of the programme for the 2nd leg of the Football League Cup semi-final, played at White Hart Lane on 23 December. In front of a 29,982 crowd, Spurs won the game 2-0 after extra time.

OFFICIAL PROGRAMME
Price ONE SHILLING (5p)

FOOTBALL LEAGUE CUP
SEMI-FINAL, 2nd LEG

TOTTENHAM HOTSPUR
v.
BRISTOL CITY

Wednesday, 23rd Dec. 1970
KICK-OFF 7.30 p.m.

SEASON 1970-71
Vol. 63   No. 35

Bristol City *v.* Millwall, 1970/71. Chris Garland (left) waits for his chance during a 3-2 home win on 20 February that lifted City out of the relegation zone. The Millwall players are 'keeper Brian King and no. 4 Alan Dorney.

Above: Bristol City *v.* Bolton Wanderers, 1970/71. A determined Gordon Parr beats a Bolton forward to the ball during City's 1-1 home draw in front of 10,550 fans on 6 March.

Right: Welcome to Ashton Gate, 1970/71. City coach John Sillett poses with loan signings Les Wilson (left) and Brian Hill on the eve of their highly praised debuts at Watford. The temporary signings of Wilson from Wolverhampton Wanderers and Hill (Coventry) were crucial in saving City from relegation.

Above: Bristol City *v.* Swindon Town, 1970/71. The visitors were beaten 2-1 in this Second Division game which was played on 20 March in front of a 17,310 (£4,346.80) crowd. No 6 is Swindon's Stan Harland, whilst City's No 9 is John Galley.

Right: Bristol City *v.* Swindon Town, 1970/71. John Galley has his close-range shot blocked by Swindon goalkeeper Peter Downsborough in the first half of the League encounter at Ashton Gate on 20 March.

Below right: Bristol City *v.* Swindon Town, 1970/71. Chris Garland (right) watches as John Galley's rasping shot puts City two up in the 53rd minute.

Bristol City *v*. Sheffield United 1970/71. City's Chris Garland is challenged by United's David Ford, watched by Trevor Hockey (left) and Brian Drysdale (right). City lost this game 1-0 in front of a 14,999 crowd who paid receipts of £3,337.15 on 27 March. At this point in the season, City were struggling down in 19th place in the Second Division table.

Bristol City *v*. Sheffield United, 1970/71. Further action from the League game against the Blades shows Les Wilson, on loan from Wolves, watching anxiously as Gordon Parr challenges United's Tony Currie.

Bristol City programmes, 1970/71 and 1971/72. *Left:* The style of the 1970/71 issue as shown by this example for the League game with Sheffield United on 27 March was the same as the previous year, though again appearing with a different front cover picture every game. The picture on this cover shows Gerry Gow heading City into a 47th minute lead against Swindon a week earlier. *Right:* A new design for 1971/72, as shown by this issue for the League game with Middlesbrough on 28 August. The Richard Hudd photograph on the cover shows John Galley scoring the opening goal in the 12th minute to set up City's outstanding 5-1 triumph against Sheffield Wednesday at Hillsborough the previous Saturday in front of a crowd of 12,724.

Left: Total commitment and tremendous enthusiasm was what you got from Gordon Parr, a highly popular player. After completing his National Service in the RAF, he had to wait a long time before cementing a regular place in the City side during the early 1960s. He helped City win promotion in 1964/65 and was a mainstay of the side until he left to join Waterford at the end of the 1971/72 season. *Right:* Once described by City boss Alan Dicks as his best ever signing, John Galley was an inelegant but effective goalscorer. Strong in the air and ungainly but deceptive on the ground, Galley's record for City was admirable given that the team were so often battling against relegation. The ex-Wolves player was signed from Rotherham United for £25,000 during 1967/68, and his goals undoubtedly saved City from relegation that season at the expense of his old club. Forest paid £30,000 for his transfer in December 1972, and thereafter he played for Peterborough United before joining Hereford United, with whom he won a Third Division Championship medal.

Personality of the week

Born
Bristol

Age
22

Previous club
Stockwood Wanderers

Signed
apprentice — 1963
full-time — 1965

Debut
v. Carlisle (home)
September 2nd, 1967

Countries played in
Spain, Germany, Holland,
France

Honours
England Schoolboys 1963

Most memorable match
v. Luton Town last season
when 2-0 down at half-time
and won the game 3-2

Ambition
To be a success with City
and play First Division
football

Married
No

Other sports
squash, swimming

Player most admired
Johnny Giles (Leeds Un.)

Appearances to start of
season
68

Goals
2

No. 2 — TREVOR TAINTON

Left: Trevor Tainton, often one of City's unsung heroes, featured as 'Personality of the Week' in City's programme for the game against Middlesbrough which was won 2-1 in front of a 16,474 crowd on 28 August 1971. A skilful winger-cum-midfielder, Tainton's dynamic play served City well with over 500 League and Cup appearances between 1967 and 1982. The crisis of 1982 brought a move to Torquay, where he played 19 games.

Below left: Gary Collier, City's cultured central defender, provoked some of City's problems when he became the first player to move under freedom of contract. After joining Coventry City in 1977/78, his League career stuttered to a halt and he moved abroad to play in America.

Centre: Les Wilson's terrific performances whilst on loan from Wolves in 1970/71 inspired City's escape from the jaws of relegation. Unfortunately, he was never quite so effective following his transfer in November 1971.

Right: Very much a raw youngster when he broke into the City side following Kellard's departure in 1970, Gerry Gow developed into one of the most influential players at Ashton Gate. Transferred to Manchester City in October 1980, this Scottish Under-23 international was a member of their FA Cup final side at the end of the season. He subsequently played for Rotherham and Burnley, before having a two-year stint as manager of Yeovil.

Green 'Un, 1971/72. The local sports paper shows City at the head of Second Division affairs following their 4-0 win in front of a 16,659 Ashton Gate crowd on 11 September.

Swindon Town *v*. Bristol City, 1971/72. Dickie Rooks (in white) breaks up the Swindon wall and Ken Wimshurst's free-kick deflects to City's No 8 Peter Spiring. In the 79th minute, Spiring scored the only goal of the game in front of a 21,595 County ground crowd. This win (on 2 October) kept City in the runners-up spot in the Second Division table.

Bristol City *v*. Watford, 1971/72. John Galley is shown scoring City's second goal in the 53rd minute as the Robin's clinched a 2-1 win against Watford in front of a 18,100 (£4,877.60) crowd at a sunny Ashton Gate on 9 October.

Bristol City, 1972/73. Left to right, back row: Trevor Tainton, Ray Cashley, Len Bond, Keith Fear. Middle row: John Sillett (coach), Alan Dicks (manager), Gerry Sweeney, John Galley, David Bruton, David Rodgers, David Merrington, John Emanuel, Les Bardsley (physiotherapist), Ken Wimshurst (coach). Front row: Brian Drysdale, Peter Spiring, Gerry Gow, Geoff Merrick, Les Wilson, Danny Bartley, Trevor Jacobs.

Above left: Keith Fear was a talented forward who played for England Boys, scoring in a 7-1 win over Wales at Reading, before making his City debut in 1970/71. Never a prolific goalscorer, but often an important one, his superb equaliser against Leeds in the FA Cup in 1974 is often fondly recalled, as is his late goal at Eastville in December 1974. After leaving City in 1977, he played for Hereford, Blackburn, Plymouth, Brentford and Chester before retiring in 1980.

Above centre: Tom Ritchie signed from Bridgend Thistle in July 1969, and this Edinburgh-born striker served City well for over a decade. He scored many important goals when City returned to the top flight after a 65-year absence, but relegation brought a transfer to Sunderland in January 1981. With City in the Fourth Division, he returned to Ashton Gate two years later and put in a couple of excellent seasons before a surprise move to Yeovil.

Above right: Given a free transfer by his first club Celtic, Gerry Sweeney came to Ashton Gate during the close season of 1971 when City paid Greenock Morton £22,000 for his services. This proved to be money well spent as over a ten-year period, this skilful defender and midfielder played in all but 32 of 478 League and Cup games. He moved on to York in February 1982 and during 1984/85 became manager at Clevedon Town. In August 1986 he was appointed assistant manager at Walsall. He has subsequently had a spell as assistant at Ashton Gate, as well as being caretaker boss for a time during 1997.

Right: Les Bardsley, City's popular physiotherapist, is pictured putting a player through his paces at Ashton Gate. From 1955, this ex-Bury midfielder was with City for over 20 years.

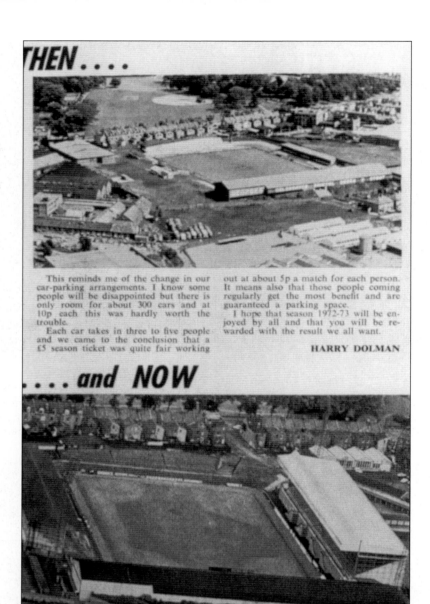

THEN . . . .

This reminds me of the change in our car-parking arrangements. I know some people will be disappointed but there is only room for about 300 cars and at 10p each this was hardly worth the trouble.

Each car takes in three to five people and we came to the conclusion that a £5 season ticket was quite fair working out at about 5p a match for each person. It means also that those people coming regularly get the most benefit and are guaranteed a parking space.

I hope that season 1972-73 will be enjoyed by all and that you will be rewarded with the result we all want.

HARRY DOLMAN

. . . . and NOW

Above: Ashton Gate. Two aerial views of the ground, which appeared in the programme for the Millwall game on 19 August 1972. The 1949 picture (top), contrasts with the 1972 view (bottom).

Right: Bristol City's Player of the Year Award, 1972/73. Player of the Year John Emanuel (left) receives the trophy from Geoff Merrick, the previous winner. This award was instigated in 1970/71, when it was won by Gerry Sharpe.

Portsmouth *v.* Bristol City, 1972/73. The City players discuss tactics at Ashton Gate prior to their FA Cup match at Pompey. From left to right, back row: Danny Bartley, Peter Spiring, Tom Ritchie, Gerry Gow, Dave Bruton, John Emanuel, Bobby Gould, Geoff Merrick, John Sillett (coach). Front row: Gerry Sweeney, Brian Drysdale, Brian Hall, David Rodgers, Trevor Tainton, Alan Dicks (manager). The talk must have worked because Bobby Gould notched a last minute goal on 13 January to secure a replay.

Bristol City *v.* Portsmouth, 1972/73. In front of a 16,699-strong crowd, Gerry Gow hits the net with his 89th minute spot kick as City beat Pompey 4-1 in this FA Cup third round replay on 16 January.

Left: Sheffield Wednesday *v.* Bristol City, 1972/73. City's Peter Spiring has a difficult time in the snow at Hillsborough in front of a crowd of 11,195. This Second Division game was abandoned after 55 minutes due to adverse conditions on 20 January when the score was 0-0.

Below: Young Robins Club, 1972/73. The members of Bristol City's Young Robins Club, which started in 1967, meet with Trevor Tainton, Danny Bartley, Geoff Merrick and Brian Drysdale at Ashton Gate.

Sunderland *v.* Bristol City, 1972/73. This action from the 2-2 draw in front of a 33,255 Roker Park crowd on 31 March shows City's David Rodgers challenging for the ball, watched by Geoff Merrick (left) and Tom Ritchie (centre).

Sunderland *v.* Bristol City, 1972/73. Further action from Roker Park as Tom Ritchie watches Geoff Merrick get in one of his renowned sliding tackles.

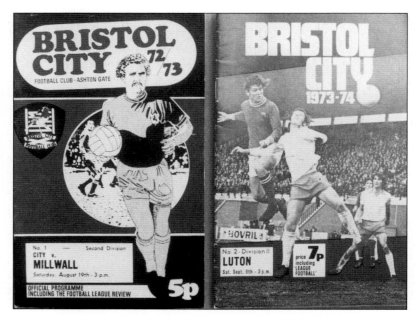

Bristol City programmes from 1972/73 and 1973/74. *Left:* The 1972/73 campaign brought a return to the wasted space of a never changing front cover, although the cartoon design showing captain Geoff Merrick and City's new badge is impressive enough. *Right:* We're back to real life in 1973/74 as this issue for the League clash with Luton Town on 8 September shows. However, the fans had to put up with this rather uninspiring picture of David Rodgers heading for goal throughout the whole campaign.

Below left: Bristol City v. Bolton Wanderers, 1973/74. City's Geoff Merrick (No 3) leaps high to beat Bolton defenders Peter Nicholson and Don McAllister to the ball. Thanks to Bobby Gould's seventh minute goal, City won this, their opening League game of the season, in front of a 13,665 Ashton Gate crowd, who paid receipts of £4,962.34 on 25 August.

Below: Bristol City v. Luton Town, 1973/74. In front of a 12,208 strong crowd, who paid receipts of £4,092.70, Bobby Gould, with his first penalty in League football, beats Graham Horn from the spot in the 39th minute of City's 3-1 home defeat on 8 September.

Bristol City *v.* Luton Town, 1973/74. This further action from the Luton game on 8 September shows Geoff Merrick and David Rodgers going for the ball.

SOCCER HOMES   *BRISTOL CITY*

Ashton Gate, home of City since the turn of the century, has a capacity set at 39,000 with seating for 7,577. The new Dolman Stand, flanking one side of the ground incorporates an indoor bowling arena and refreshment rooms. Inset: City manager Alan Dicks.

Soccer homes – Ashton Gate, 1973/74. In this view of Ashton Gate, which appeared in the *Football League Review*, it can be seen that the Dolman Stand, which opened in 1970, differs from what was originally proposed above in that two ends were revised and the pillars omitted. Note in this picture the distinctive angled heads of City's second floodlighting system. These lights, which were first switched on for the Wolves game on 28 December 1965, when a 36,184 crowd (£7,302.15.0) saw City lose 1-0, remained at Ashton Gate until they were dismantled in the summer of 1992.

Above: Preston North End *v.* Bristol City, 1973/74. Keith Fear heads in City's 78th minute equaliser in front of a 10,790 crowd at Deepdale on 15 September.

Right: Preston North End *v.* Bristol City, 1973/74. A prone Keith Fear is congratulated by Tom Ritchie (8) and Bobby Gould following his headed equaliser at Deepdale on 15 September.

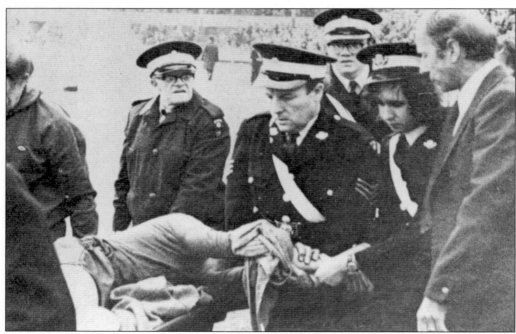

Preston North End *v.* Bristol City 1973/74. The Preston 'keeper Alan Kelly was even more in the wars however, as he sustained a dislocated shoulder. This picture shows him being stretchered off with his concerned manager, Bobby Charlton, in attendance.

Millwall *v*. Bristol City, 1973/74. Bobby Gould fires in City's 68th minute opener in front of a Cold Blow Lane crowd of 7,543 on 13 October.

Millwall *v*. Bristol City, 1973/74. Clive Whitehead notches up City's second goal just a minute after Gould had found the back of the net. The New Cross greyhound stadium can be seen in the background.

Millwall *v*. Bristol City, 1973/74. Further action from the Den on 13 October shows Millwall's Barry Kitchener keeping Donnie Gillies at bay.

Bristol City *v*. Coventry City, 1973/74. Bobby Gould is congratulated after scoring in front of the 19,196 Ashton Gate fans who witnessed an exhilarating 2-2 draw in the third round of the Football League Cup on 30 October. Unfortunately, City lost the replay 2-1 seven days later in front of a crowd of 13,049.

Hereford United *v.* Bristol City, 1973/74. Donnie Gillies illustrates just how muddy the conditions were at Edgar Street for this FA Cup fourth round clash which City won 1-0, thanks to Geoff Merrick's 17th minute goal, in front of 17,431 fans on 26 January.

Bristol City *v.* Cardiff City, 1973/74. The Robins beat the Bluebirds 3-2 in front of a 24,487 crowd on 2 February. The City players are Gillies (9), Gow and Merrick. For Cardiff, Carlin is in the number 10 shirt, whilst on the extreme right is Murray.

CITY'S FINEST HOUR

LEEDS 0, CITY 1—the greatest result for the club for 53 years.

Top—The happy dressing room scene after the triumph.

Centre—A brilliant saving tackle by GEOFF MERRICK on BILLY BREMNER near the end.

Left — Goalscorer DONNIE GILLIES is congratulated by GEOFF and chief coach JOHN SILLETT at the end.

Leeds United *v*. Bristol City, 1973/74. Action from City's 1-0 victory in a fifth round replay at Elland Road on 9 March 1974. A crowd of 47,182 (£38,283) saw a 73rd minute Donnie Gillies goal bring City their greatest FA Cup triumph.

Three
Pride before the Fall

Bristol City, 1974/75. From left to right, back row: Ken Wimshurst (coach), John Emanuel, Donnie Gillies, Paul Cheesley, John Bond, John Shaw, Ray Cashley, David Rodgers, Garry Collier, Tom Ritchie, Les Bardsley (physiotherapist). Front row: Keith Fear, Mike Brolly, Ernie Hunt, Trevor Tainton, Geoff Merrick, Alan Dicks (manager), Brian Drysdale, Jimmy Mann, Gerry Sweeney, Gerry Gow, Clive Whitehead.

Bristol City *v.* Manchester United, 1974/75. City's John Emanuel turns in triumph after scoring City's 31st minute winning goal in front of 28,104 Ashton Gate fans, who paid receipts of £12,991.72 on 9 November. City achieved a notable double over the Champions this season as a last-minute strike by Donnie Gillies was to bring success in front of a 47,118 Old Trafford crowd on 1 February.

Bristol City *v.* Manchester United, 1974/75. Further action from this game shows City's Tom Ritchie beating Arnold Sidebottom to get in his header.

Right: Bristol City *v.* Aston Villa, 1974/75. Paul Cheesley jumps in at Villa 'keeper Jim Cumbes, with John Robson close by. City won this game 1-0 in front of a 13,390 (£4,536.30) Ashton Gate crowd on 7 December.

Below: Bristol Rovers *v.* Bristol City, 1974/75. Keith Fear holds his arms aloft in the 58th minute after scoring City's equaliser at Eastville on 28 December. With the wind in their favour after the break, City stormed back from a half-time deficit to win 4-1 in front of a 20,911 crowd.

Left: Bristol City *v.* West Bromwich Albion, 1974/75. Referee Clive Thomas is perhaps checking to see if City's Keith Fear needs assistance in doing up his laces.

Below: Bristol City *v.* West Bromwich Albion, 1974/75. On 22 February, Keith Fear certainly needed no help in scoring City's 79th minute winner, his perfect chip (arguably one of the best goals of the 1970s) helped City achieve an exciting 2-1 Second Division success in front of 14,180 fans, who paid receipts of £5,206.75. This result took the side up to fifth place.

Bristol City *v*. Bristol Rovers, 1974/75. Despite dominating this Second Division encounter, City could only manage a 1-1 draw in front of the 28,953 Ashton Gate crowd who paid receipts of £13,449.73 on 1 April. In this picture, City's Mike Brolly watches Gerry Sweeney getting in his shot on goal, despite the attentions of Graham Day and 'keeper Jim Eadie. After losing at home to Norwich in the previous match, this was a further blow to City's promotion aspirations as they remained in fifth spot.

Bristol City programme, 1974/75 and 1975/76. There is quite a contrast between these two issues. *Left:* Back to the larger size issues (9" x 7") of the 1954/55 and 1955/56 era as shown by this 24-page production for the League clash with Nottingham Forest on 14 December. Unfortunately, this season marked the end of the *Football League Review*. *Right:* The fans were surprised in 1975/76 by this unusually sized (7.5" x 4") 24-page production which, as this illustration shows, first appeared for the home League game with Bolton Wanderers on 16 August.

THE PROMOTION SQUAD
1975-76

Bristol City, 1975/76. This squad took Bristol City back into the top flight after an absence of 65 years. From left to right, back row: Donnie Gillies, Ray Cashley, John Shaw, Clive Whitehead. Middle row: Alan Dicks (manager), Paul Cheesley, David Rodgers, Tom Ritchie, Garry Collier, Ken Wimshust (chief coach), Les Bardsley (physiotherapist). Front row: Mike Brolly, Jimmy Mann, Brian Drysdale, Geoff Merrick, Trevor Tainton, Gerry Sweeney, Gerry Gow.

Bristol City v. York City, 1975/76. Tom Ritchie beats the 'keeper before slotting in one of his three goals in a 4-1 League success on 22 November.

Bristol City *v*. York City, 1975/76. Further action from this game, the highlights of which were shown on BBC's Match of the Day. The Dolman Stand provides an imposing backdrop as Jimmy Mann (left) and Tom Ritchie (right) watch Geoff Merrick's diving header. Whilst the 11,228 crowd, paying receipts of £5,720.15, were thrilled by City's success, which kept them in third place, many were impressed by the attack-minded inclinations of the lowly visitors.

Bristol City *v*. Plymouth Argyle, 1975/76. Geoff Merrick's superb flying header brings City their first equaliser in the 35th minute of this thrilling Boxing Day encounter. A 2-2 draw in front of a 21,471 crowd (£14,456.48) in this Second Division game kept City in third place.

Bristol City v. Plymouth Argyle, 1975/76. Further action from the Boxing Day encounter with the Pilgrims shows City's Tom Ritchie going for goal.

Coventry City v. Bristol City, 1975/76. Mike Brolly fires in City's 78th minute goal during an unlucky 2-1 FA Cup defeat at Highfield Road in front of a 15,653 crowd on 3 January.

Oxford United *v.* Bristol City, 1975/76. On 10 January against bottom of the table Oxford, and in front of 7,594 crowd, it seemed that it was going to be so easy when Paul Cheesley put City in front with this header early on. By the finish, however, the Robin's were grateful for 'keeper Ray Cashley's superb display, which brought them a point in a 1-1 draw.

Bristol City *v.* Blackburn Rovers, 1975/76. Jimmy Mann (far right) shoots in the sixth minute winner at the Covered End. A crowd of 12,168 (£6,329.85) attended this Second Division game, which City won 1-0 on 17 January.

Left: Bristol City *v*. Southampton, 1975/76. Paul Cheesley in action during the 1-1 home draw, in front of a 22,316 (£14,869.82) crowd on 7 February.

Below: Bristol City *v*. Southampton, 1975/76. City's Brian Drysdale in action during the vital clash with the Saints on 7 February.

Bristol City *v.* Portsmouth, 1975/76. The celebrations after City beat Pompey 1-0, in front of a 27,394 Ashton Gate crowd, to clinch promotion on the evening of 20 April.

ALL IN THE GAME

Three in the ring (left) — Tom Ritchie, Donnie Gillies and Gerry Gow in action during the television contest against Manchester United.

Beat the Wall (below) — the five-man human wall keeping the Derby County shots out in the semi-final (being televised tomorrow) — Tom Ritchie, Gerry Gow, Geoff Merrick, Gerry Sweeney and Donnie Gillies.

Above: Bristol City *v.* Notts County, 1975/76. City hoped to end their promotion campaign by beating Notts, but the visitors were not prepared to be sacrificial lambs. Despite Gow's diving header, the Magpies pulled off a 2-1 success in front of a 24,614 (£16,169.75) Ashton Gate crowd on 24 April.

Left: All In The Game, 1976. Devised by City boss Alan Dicks this, the second All In The Game soccer skills contest, took place at Ashton Gate over the weekend of 17 and 18 July. The top picture is of City's 230-210 success over Manchester United in front of a Saturday crowd of 7,000. The bottom picture shows action from the semi-final against Derby County, with City's five-man human wall attempting to keep out their opponents shots in front of a 10,000 crowd on 18 July. Alas, the Rams won by 210 points to 195 to progress to final, where they defeated Norwich City 290-255. The first contest was held in 1974, and the third and final one in 1977.

Promotion, 1975/76. City manager Alan Dicks (left) and striker Paul Cheesley (centre) at a
Sportsman's Dinner with the great Welsh rugby fly-half Cliff Morgan.

All In The Game, 1976. The
programme for the soccer skills contest
All in the Game, held during the
summer of 1976.

Arsenal *v*. Bristol City, 1976/77. On 21 August City produced a scintillating performance to mark their return to the top flight. They fully deserved their success at Highbury, although the 1-0 scoreline, courtesy of Paul Cheesley's 65th minute header, did them scant justice in front of a 41,082 crowd, who generated receipts of £31,643.33. The photograph shows Clive Whitehead putting in a shot at the Clock End during the second half.

Arsenal *v*. Bristol City, 1976/77. Further action from Highbury shows City players (from left to right) Tainton, Merrick and Sweeney.

Above: Arsenal *v.* Bristol City, 1976/77. Jimmy Mann watches as City's Gary Collier makes an aerial challenge for the ball with Arsenal's John Radford.

Right: Bristol City programme, 1976/77. The large-style format was back in vogue this season, as shown by this issue for the Stoke City game on 24 August.

PROMOTED TO DIVISION ONE 1976

BRISTOL CITY

FIRST HOME MATCH BACK IN DIVISION
ONE FOR 65 YEARS

versus

STOKE CITY

Bristol City's first match back
in Division 1 was 'away' at
Arsenal.
RESULT
Arsenal 0 Bristol City 1
(Cheesely)

MATCH RESULT
BRISTOL C. 1 STOKE C. 1
(Gillies)   (Smith)

The Secretary
Bristol City F.C.
Ashton Gate
Bristol BS3 2EJ

Opposite above: Bristol City *v.* Stoke City, 1976/77. This first day cover was produced to mark City's first home match back in the top flight. In front of a 25,316 crowd, who paid receipts of £15,948.93, City drew 1-1 with Stoke. Unfortunately, during the game, Paul Cheesley sustained the injury that was to end his career.

Opposite below: Bristol City *v.* Leeds United, 1976/77. City in the fog at Ashton Gate, pictured on the attack, from left to right Tom Ritchie, Clive Whitehead and Jimmy Mann. This game, played on 4 December in front of 30,491 supporters (£19,082.05), was abandoned at half time because of poor visibility.

Above: Bristol City *v.* Everton, 1976/77. Norman Hunter clears off the line at home to Everton on 5 March. A 21,108 crowd, who generated receipts of £11,977.58, witnessed this vital game which City lost 2-1, despite taking a second minute lead when Peter Cormack put away a penalty at the Open End. This result put City down in 21st place.

Left: Bristol City programme, 1977/78. The large format was retained for this campaign, but yet again the photographs on the cover remained unchanged throughout the season. This League Cup clash with Stoke City on 29 August was won 1-0 in front of 11,877 spectators, who realised receipts of £12,959.39.

69

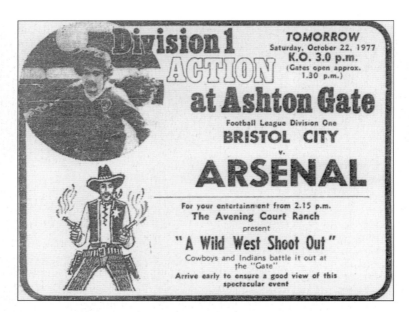

Bristol City *v*. Arsenal, 1977/78. Advertisement from the *Bristol Evening Post* for the match at Ashton Gate on 22 October.

Bristol City *v*. Arsenal, 1977/78. The Wild West Show provided the pre-match entertainment at Ashton Gate on the occasion of Arsenal's visit. Unfortunately, the Gunners came with firing power of their own as they achieved a 2-0 success in front of the 24,864 crowd, who generated receipts of £16,962.45. This picture shows Geoff Merrick leading out the City side, followed by Gerry Sweeney and Tom Ritchie.

Bristol City *v*. St Mirren, 1977/78. Gerry Sweeney and Kevin Mabbutt are holding the Anglo-Scottish Cup. A 1-1 draw with St Mirren in front of a 16,110 Ashton Gate crowd on 5 December was good enough for City to take the Cup 3-2 on aggregate.

Bristol City *v*. Newcastle United, 1977/78. Tom Ritchie bursts between two Newcastle defenders during City's 3-1 home success in front of 17,142 fans (£9,531) on 1 April.

Left: The Rockin' Robins, 1978/79. City's cheerleaders, who supplied the pre-match entertainment during City's First Division sojourn, are shown on the front cover of this programme for the game against Spurs on 13 January (which was drawn 0-0 in front of a 22,767 crowd).

Below: Bristol City *v.* Bristol Rovers, 1978/79. Scottish international Peter Cormack steers his penalty past Rovers 'keeper Martin Thomas in front of 9,874 Ashton Gate fans on 5 August as City move towards a famous 6-1 Anglo-Scottish triumph.

PETER CORMACK carefully steers his penalty past Bristol Rovers goalkeeper MARTIN THOMAS as City move towards a 6-1 Anglo-Scottish Cup victory.

Chris Garland heads the sixth goal over the line in the Anglo-Scottish Cup clash with Bristol Rovers, watched by a forlorn Phil Bater.

Bristol City *v*. Bristol Rovers 1978/79. Further action from the Anglo-Scottish Cup clash shows City's Chris Garland almost on the line as he heads in the sixth goal.

Bristol City programmes from 1978/79 and 1979/80. *Left:* The opening home League game with Norwich heralded this slightly smaller programme. This seemed a poor product for a top flight club, especially with the number of pages being reduced to sixteen. *Right:* Perhaps to make up for the previous year, City came up with this brilliant programme for 1979/80. This example for the opening game versus Leeds on 18 August, which marked a return to standard sized issues, set the benchmark for the season, which saw City romp away with the best programme award.

Left: Birmingham City *v.* Bristol City, 1979/80. Tom Ritchie gets the final touch to Geert Meyer's corner during City's 4-0 Anglo-Scottish Cup win in front of a 7,691 St Andrew's crowd on 4 August. *Right:* The Gillette Cup, 1979. The Somerset captain Brian Rose is pictured on the Ashton Gate pitch holding the Gillette Cup with City's Gerry Gow on the occasion of the Nottingham Forest game which was drawn 1-1 in front of a 22,767 crowd on 22 September.

Aston Villa *v.* Bristol City, 1979/80. This picture, showing Kevin Mabbutt on the ball, with other City players, Gerry Gow (left) and Gerry Sweeney (centre), during City's 2-0 win at Villa Park in front of a 25,526 crowd on 25 August, appeared on the cover of the programme for the Ipswich game on 26 January.

Crystal Palace *v.* Bristol City, 1979/80. Only an acrobatic leap by Paul Hinshelwood, the son of former City winger Wally, denies Joe Royle from scoring in the 1-1 draw at Selhurst Park in front of a 27,499 crowd on 20 October.

Crystal Palace *v.* Bristol City, 1979/80. Royle isn't denied for long however, as is shown by expression on the face on Kenny Sansom and keeper John Burridge. A through ball by Tony Fitzpatrick allowed Royle to put City in front in the 67th minute of this First Division game, even though he was injured in the process.

SPOT ON! Gerry Gow puts City into the lead from this penalty.

Gerry is called on again to take City's second spot kick against Brighton and duly obliges with another goal.

Bristol City *v.* Brighton and Hove Albion, 1979/80. Gerry Gow had his shooting boots on in this First Division clash with Brighton, as these two pictures demonstrate. His two penalties in front of a 19,896 (£18,498.65) crowd on New Year's Day brought City a draw.

Bristol City, 1979/80. This squad wasn't strong enough to keep City among the elite.

Bristol City *v.* Derby County, 1979/80. Action from the FA Cup clash played on 5 January. Note the Tobacco Bond Warehouses on the left, which were demolished in February 1995. City won this third round game 6-2 in front of a 13,384 crowd.

Bristol City *v.* Derby County 1979/80. Further action from City's 6-2 FA Cup success; this time, Chris Garland is scoring for City.

Bristol City *v.* Liverpool, 1979/80. Even the best efforts of Liverpool's Alan Hansen on the line cannot stop Kevin Mabbutt's shot from entering the net. Unfortunately, this 63rd minute goal wasn't enough for City who slumped to a 3-1 defeat in front of 27,523 home fans on 15 March.

The Charles Tew Memorial Trophy, 1979/80. Although relegated from the top flight, City won the award for best match-day programme in the Football League. This programme for the game against Middlesbrough, which was won 3-1 on 22 April, shows City's Commercial manager, Jim Evans, with the trophy the club won for sweeping the board in all five categories. They became only the second club, after Leeds United, to top all five sections – (i) most improved; (ii) best value; (iii) most attractive cover; (iv) best in the First Division; (v) best in the whole League – voted on by the Programme Club since the award was first instigated in 1966 when Arsenal were the winners. The trophy was named after a Programme Club member who was killed in a car accident when travelling home following an England *v.* Scotland match at Wembley in 1973.

Bristol City *v.* Norwich City, 1979/80. In front of a crowd of 16,596, who paid receipts of £12,543.40 on 26 April, City were slightly unfortunate to lose this their final home game in the top flight 3-2. Here Canaries 'keeper Roger Hansbury seems amused by what the referee, Alan Seville, is saying to City's Joe Royle, who somewhat ironically moved to Norwich in the close season.

79

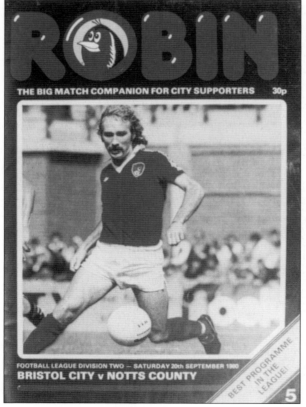

Above: Bristol City *v.* Norwich City, 1979/80. This action from the Norwich game on 26 April shows Gerry Gow shooting for goal.

Left: Bristol City programme, 1980/81. The comment on this programme's cover for the game versus Notts County, which was lost 1-0 in front of 8,253 fans on 20 September, relates to the award for the previous season's effort. However, somewhat surprisingly, this season's larger sized (9.5" x 6.75") offering was still considered good enough to secure the Second Division award.

Bristol City *v*. Swansea City, 1980/81.
A fine action photograph of Clive Whitehead
in an aerial challenge with Swansea's Robbie
James during a 1-0 home defeat watched by
9,761 fans on 6 September.

Bob Houghton and Stephen Kew,
1980/81. City's new boss Bob
Houghton (left), who lead Swedish
club Malmo to the European Cup
final in 1978/79, pictured with
City chairman Stephen Kew.

Bristol City *v.* Derby County, 1980/81. Kevin Mabbutt scores for City in the 2-2 draw with Derby County in front of 12,049 (£11,377.70) Ashton Gate fans on 25 October.

Bristol City *v.* Oldham Athletic, 1980/81. In front of a 8,485 Ashton Gate crowd on 29 November, Chris Garland watches in the background as Kevin Mabbutt runs to congratulate Tony Fitzpatrick on scoring City's 53rd minute equaliser.

Bristol City *v.* Chelsea, 1980/81. The safe hands of City's Jan Moller break up another Chelsea attack during the goal-less home draw in front of 10,011 (£9,013.50) fans on 18 April.

Bristol City programme, 1981/82. There were two different styles of programme for this season. *Left:* The campaign started with an abysmal offering with the manager's comments on the front cover, as shown by this 8-page issue for the League game versus Doncaster Rovers on 5 September. *Right:* Later in the campaign, from 23 January, a coloured cover was introduced as shown by this issue for the first game of the Bristol City (1982) organisation against Fulham on 6 February – but this gave even less value for money, it not being thought fit to increase the number of pages to compensate for the loss of the front-page blurb.

Above: Bristol City *v.* Doncaster Rovers, 1981/82. A typical action picture of Mick Hartford, but this time his header was off target in City's 2-2 home draw in front of 6,996 (£7,699.80) fans on 5 September.

Left: Bristol City *v.* Chesterfield, 1981/82. City's new boy Terry Boyle in action during his debut in the goal-less draw with Chesterfield watched by 8,110 (£8,940.10) Ashton Gate fans on 31 October. The Welsh international defender was valued at £100,000 in the exchange, which took Kevin Mabbutt to Crystal Palace.

Lessons of History. Whilst from an earlier era, this Bob Bennett cartoon, from the *Bristol Evening Post* of 1 August 1933, illustrates the crisis that Bristol City faced in 1982, almost fifty years after the events it was originally drawn to portray.

Newport County *v.* Bristol City, 1981/82. Mike Harford (centre) scores in City's 1-1 draw in front of a 5,915 crowd at Somerton Park on 30 January, and skipper Terry Boyle looks to congratulate him. The City fans who travelled to this game were fearful that it would be the club's last. Fortunately, with certain players (the Ashton Gate Eight) accepting a redundancy offer just before the deadline a few days later, Bristol City (1982) PLC was formed.

Bristol City *v.* Fulham, 1981/82. With City saved, subject to a new share issue, 9,312 turned out on 6 February to witness a 0-0 draw with the promotion-chasing visitors.

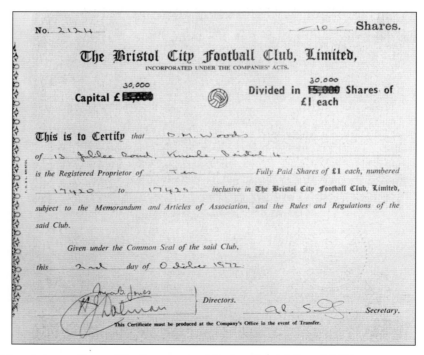

No. 2124   10   **Shares.**

The Bristol City Football Club, Limited,
INCORPORATED UNDER THE COMPANIES' ACTS.

Capital £ ~~15,000~~ 30,000   **Divided in** ~~15,000~~ 30,000 **Shares of £1 each**

This is to Certify *that* D. M. Woods

of 13 Jubilee Road, Knowle, Bristol 4

is the Registered Proprietor of Ten *Fully Paid Shares of £1 each, numbered* 17420 *to* 17429 *inclusive in* The Bristol City Football Club, Limited, *subject to the Memorandum and Articles of Association, and the Rules and Regulations of the said Club.*

Given under the Common Seal of the said Club,

this 2nd *day of* October 1972.

         } *Directors.*   *Secretary.*

This Certificate must be produced at the Company's Office in the event of Transfer.

Bristol City share certificate. The formation of the new Bristol City (1982) organisation rendered the old share certificates worthless.

Bristol City *v*. Exeter City, 1981/82. In the 30th minute, Mick Harford scores City's second goal in front of 6,617 (£8,118.90) fans during the 3-2 home win over Exeter on 23 February.

City's Alan Nicholls gets the better of Rovers' Archie Stevens.

Bristol City *v*. Bristol Rovers, 1981/82. City's Alan Nicholls gets the better of Rovers' Archie Stevens during the 2-1 home defeat in front of 11,451 (£14,396.70) fans on 12 April.

The Rolling Stones, 1982. The Rolling Stones concert on 26 June 1982 attracted what has proved to be the largest crowd (35,123) in the history of the new Bristol City 1982 PLC organisation at Ashton Gate.

Four

New Beginnings

Bristol City, 1982/83. Back row, from left to right: Alex Lockhart (physiotherapist), Paul Stevens, Gary Williams, Jon Economou, John Shaw, Garry Smith, Russell Musker, Wayne Bray, Terry Cooper (player/manager). Front row: Steve Thompson, Ricky Chandler, Alan Nicholls, Terry Boyle, Tom Ritchie, Robert Newman, Alan Crawford, Glyn Riley.

Bristol City programme, 1982/83. Two differing styles for the standard sized issue produced this season, the change being made from the Port Vale game on 27 December. *Left:* This game, which was won 1-0 against Torquay United in the Group Cup on 17 August, only attracted a 1,421 crowd to Ashton Gate. *Right:* Darlington proved a bigger attraction on 2 May with 4,877 (£5,117.05) turning up to see a 2-2 draw.

Bristol City Reserves, 1982/83. Back row, left to right: Kevin Slabber, Omele Kelly, Nyrere Kelly, Martin Grimshaw, Alan Nicholls, Ricky Chandler, Gerry Sharpe (manager). Front row: Colin Freeman, Simon Panes, Steve Thompson, Mark Jones, Steve Palmer, Andy Llewellyn.

Above left: Bristol City v. Wimbledon, 1982/83. David Beasant Wimbledon's Goalkeeper climbs above Riley.

Economou on one of his dazzling runs through the mbledon defence.

Above left: Bristol City *v.* Wimbledon, 1982/83. David Beasant, Wimbledon's gigantic 'keeper, foils Gyn Riley during City's 4-2 Ashton Gate success in front of 4,744 (£4,962.64) fans on 23 October.

Above right: Bristol City *v.* Wimbledon, 1982/83. Further action from the match with the Dons shows City's Jon Economu making one of his typically mazy dribbles.

Right: City secretary John Lillington completes the signing of Forbes Phillipson-Masters during November 1982. This proved to be a crucial capture for the new Bristol City (1982) organisation, which at the time was sinking at the foot of the Football League. He added much needed steel to City's defence, and enabled the club to gradually haul themselves out of trouble.

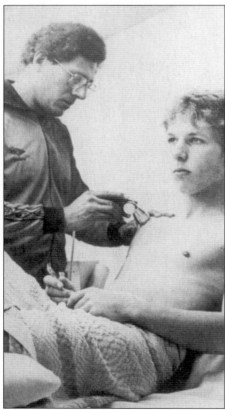

Above: Bristol City *v.* Northampton Town, 1982/83. Neil Freeman, in his farewell game before joining the police, just fails to stop Tom Ritchie's 41st minute spot-kick during City's 3-1 home defeat in front of 4,874 (£5,159.90) fans on 22 January. *Left:* Alex Lockhart, 1982/83. City's physiotherapist Lockhart who, after 22 years service in the Royal Army Medical Corps, took over from Bill Heather on 2 July 1981, treats Gary Williams. *Below:* Bristol City *v.* Barnsley, 1983/84. Alan Crawford nets with a spectacular header in City's 3-1 pre-season friendly success against Barnsley, watched by just 1,183 diehard fans at Ashton Gate on 16 August.

Alan Crawford scores his first goal against Torquay, giving City a 1-0 lead at half time.

Bristol City *v.* Torquay United, 1983/84. Alan Crawford scores the opening goal in the 41st minute of this Fourth Division game in front of an Ashton Gate crowd of 5,266 on 24 September. Alan added to his tally in the second half as City went on to win 5-0.

Right: Bristol City *v.* Peterborough United, 1983/84. Howard Pritchard holds off Peterbrough's Phillip Chard at Ashton Gate on 29 October.

Left: Manager of the Month award, 1983/84. City boss Terry Cooper with his award for being the Division Four Manager of the Month for December. Cooper was born in Leeds on 12 July 1944, and this much-capped England international played for Leeds United, Middlesbrough, Bristol City and Bristol Rovers before taking over the reins at Eastville. After being dismissed from the Rovers hot seat, he reverted to playing with Doncaster Rovers before becoming City's player/manager in May 1982.

Below: Bristol City v. Aldershot, 1983/84. The man with the longest name in British football, Forbes Phillipson-Masters (left), is challenged by Aldershot's Clive Day as he heads for goal. City won this Fourth Division game 2-1 in front of a 7,140 (£8,909.50) Ashton Gate crowd on 25 February.

Right: Bristol City *v.* Tranmere Rovers, 1983/84. Tranmere's Dai Davies thwarts City's Trevor Morgan during the 1-1 home draw, watched by 6,613 (£8,245.46) fans on 24 March.

Below: Bristol City programmes, 1983/84 and 1984/85. The fans got good value for money from the standard sized issues of both these two campaigns. *Left:* City won this FA Cup replay against the Corinthian Casuals 4-0 in front of a 5,339 attendance on 23 November. *Right:* The Rovers won this FA Cup clash, in front of a 19,367 crowd (£45,300), 3-1 on 8 December, despite Bruce Halliday heading City into a fourth minute lead.

Above: Bristol City *v.* Colchester United, 1983/84. City's Tom Ritchie sends the Colchester 'keeper Alec Chamberlain the wrong way in the 26th minute as he registers from the spot to open the scoring on 31 March.

Left: Bristol City Reserves programme, 1984/85. For the first half of this season programmes, as opposed to team sheets, were issued for Reserve games. This example is for the Western League meeting with Bideford, which was drawn 0-0 at Ashton Gate on 15 December.

Bristol City *v.* Newport County, 1984/85. With the adverse winter weather continuing, the postponement of this fixture on 12 January enabled these delightful pictures to be taken at Ashton Gate.

City's Keith Curle heads clear from Ian Rush.

Bristol City *v.* Liverpool, 1985/86. Keith Curle heads clear from Liverpool's Ian Rush in the 3-3 friendly draw with Liverpool, in front of a 8,182 Ashton Gate crowd on 10 August.

Away Action Scene at Orient

Alan Walsh finally gets the well deserved winner as he slots the ball past this Orient defender to score late in the second half.

GOAL! Alan Walsh celebrates after scoring the City winner.

Alan Walsh celebrates his goal.

Photographs by David Katz.

Bobby Hutchinson scores City's second goal v Wolves.

Opposite: Orient *v.* Bristol City, 1984/85. A three-picture sequence showing Alan Walsh's well-deserved 77th minute winner in front of a 2,754 crowd at Brisbane Road on 9 February. For the 500 City fans who travelled by train to this game it proved quite a journey, because the cold weather delayed their arrival until 30 minutes or so before the end. By way of recompense, they were offered a trip to Gillingham later in the season for just £2.

Above: Bristol City *v.* Wolverhampton Wanderers, 1985/86. Bobby Huchinson shoots in City's second goal in the 40th minute on 26 October. City went on to beat an extremely poor Wolves side 3-0 watched by a 7,138 crowd, who paid receipts of £11,581.

Right: Bristol City *v.* Wolverhampton Wanderers, 1985/86. This further action from the Wolves game shows Steve Neville looking on as Howard Pritchard is thwarted by the Wolves 'keeper Scott Barrett.

Scott Barrett saves from City's Howard Pritchard.

Bolton Wanderers *v*. Bristol City, 1985/86. Action from the Freight Rover Final at Wembley, which City won 3-0 on 24 May.

Bolton Wanderers *v*. Bristol City, 1985/86. The match-winning City team with the trophy after the game.

Bristol City programme, 1985/86 and 1986/87. *Left:* Despite the terrible cover, the programme this season offered value for money. This game against Rotherham on 11 January was won 3-1 in front of a 6,672 (£10,907.90) crowd. *Right:* The good work wasn't continued in this campaign however, as the Freight Rover Trophy winners of the previous season could only come up with a very poor offering. Newport were beaten 4-0 in front of 9,137 spectators, who paid receipts of £17,187.70, on 14 March.

Bristol City *v*. Bristol Rovers, 1986/87. Disappointment awaited City in this clash with their old rivals, as Gary Smart's late 20-yard strike won the points for the Rovers in front of a 17,122 New Year's Day Ashton Gate crowd, which generated receipts of £37,572.95.

Bristol City *v*. Doncaster Rovers, 1986/87. Doncaster's Neil Redfern is unable to prevent Alan Walsh firing in City's fourth goal in the 68th minute of a 5-0 success, watched by 8,932 Ashton Gate fans who paid receipts of £16,629.90 on 7 February.

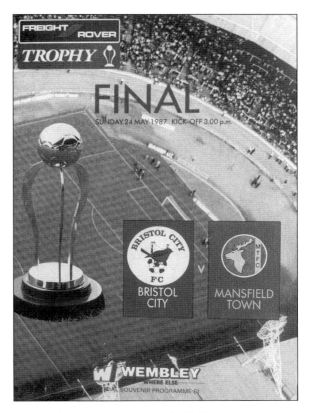

Right: Bristol City *v.* Mansfield Town 1986/87. City were hot favourites to win back to back Freight Rover Finals, but it wasn't to be. They succumbed to Mansfield, in front of a 58,586 crowd, paying receipts of £324,592, on 24 May by losing 5-4 in the very first penalty shoot-out to decide a Wembley final.

Below: Bristol City *v.* Mansfield Town, 1986/87. This action from the Freight Rover final shows the Stags 'keeper, Kevin Hancock, gathering a corner. The City players are Keith Curle (14), Joe Jordan (11) and David Moyes (4).

Left: Bristol City *v*. Southampton, 1987/88. City captain Steve Galliers in action during the 4-2 home friendly defeat in front of a 2,815 crowd on 29 July. The other City player in view is Rob Newman.

Below: Bristol City *v*. Port Vale, 1987/88. The 8,716 Ashton Gate crowd, who generated receipts of £20,213.60 on 31 August, watch Steve Neville volleying in City's 89th minute winner.

Bristol City *v*. Port Vale, 1987/88. Joe Jordan dives in where it hurts during the City's 1-0 win on 31 August.

Bristol City *v*. Chester, 1987/88. This action from the game played on 21 November shows Carl Shutt heading in City's second goal in the 68th minute. The 8,103 fans, who paid receipts of £18,328.50, witnessed a 2-2 draw.

Bristol City *v*. Torquay United, 1987/88. The antics of Torquay 'keeper Kenny Allen keeps Rob Newman at bay during City's 1-0 FA Cup second round defeat in front of a 9,027 Ashton Gate crowd on 5 December.

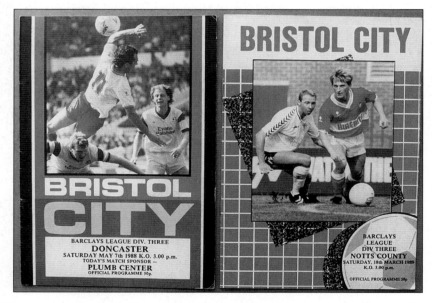

Bristol City programme 1987/88 and 1988/89. *Left:* The front cover throughout the 1987/88 campaign carried this picture of Joe Jordan flying in against Mansfield in the previous season Freight Rover Trophy Final at Wembley Stadium. This programme was issued for the vital game against Doncaster on 7 May when, in front of a 18,373 (£49,754.80) crowd, Colin Gordon's second-half strike took City through to a place in the end of season play-offs. *Right:* Steve Galliers is shown on the front cover of this issue for the game versus Notts County which was lost 4-0 in front of 6,407 fans who generated receipts of £15,357.10 on 18 March.

Bristol City *v.* Nottingham Forest, 1988/89. Forest's Stephen Hodge watches as Joe Jordan and Des Walker adopt ballet-like poise during the Football League Cup semi-final second leg game at Ashton Gate on 26 February. Forest won 1-0 after extra time in front of 28,084 spectators (£97,097) to progress through to the final.

Bristol City *v.* Northampton Town, 1988/89. Watched by a 7,197 crowd, who paid receipts of £17,744.50, the Northampton 'keeper Peter Gleasure is well beaten in the 27th minute by Carl Shutt's spectacular shot which put City in front at Ashton Gate on 4 March.

Peter Gleasure given no chance by Robbie Turner's header for City's third goal v. Northampton.

Rob Newman looks on as Swindon's Jon Gittens and City's Bob Taylor tussle for the ball.

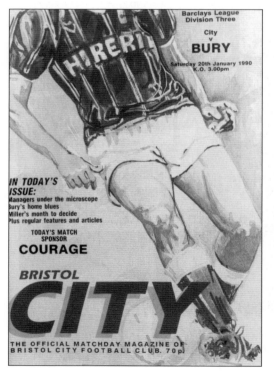

Above left: Bristol City *v.* Northampton Town, 1988/89. Further action from this Third Division game shows Robbie Turner heading in City's third goal in the 43rd minute of a 3-1 victory.

Above right: Bristol City *v.* Swindon Town, 1989/90. Rob Newman looks on as Swindon's Jon Gittens and City's Bob Taylor battle for the ball. Receipts of £44,500 were generated at this FA Cup game, which City won 2-1 in front of a 17,422 crowd on 6 January.

Left: Bristol City programme, 1989/90. Bury are beaten 1-0, thanks to Dave Smith's 35th minute shot. This game was played in front of a crowd of 10,992 on 20 January.

Five

Withering on the Vine

Two goal Bob Taylor looks on as Blackburn 'keeper Terry Gennoe and defender Kevin Moran come under pressure.

Bristol City *v.* Blackburn Rovers, 1990/91. Two-goal Bob Taylor (second left) looks on as Blackburn 'keeper Terry Gennoe comes under pressure during City's 4-2 Second Division success on 25 August watched by a 13,794 crowd, who paid receipts of £56,940.

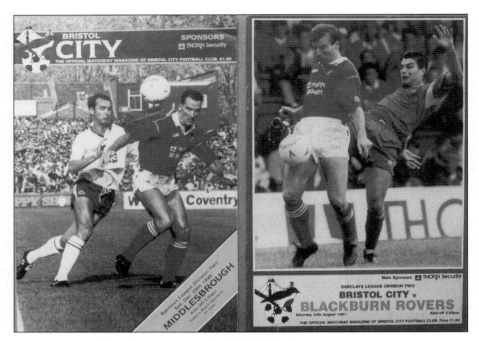

Bristol City programme 1990/91 and 1991/92. *Left:* Mark Aizlewood, who won 21 Welsh caps whilst with City, is shown on the front of this programme for the game with Middlesbrough, which was won 3-0 in front of a 14,023 (£59,605.00) crowd on 29 December. *Right:* The skilful Nicky Morgan is shown on the cover of this issue for the game which attracted 11,317 fans (£51,689.00) to see Blackburn beaten 1-0 on 24 August.

Bristol Rovers *v.* Bristol City, 1991/92. David Rennie (right) watches as Russell Osman (4) clears a Rovers attack. Unfortunately, he was unable to prevent a 3-2 defeat in front of a 6,306 Twerton Park crowd on 21 December.

Above: Bristol City *v.* Cardiff City, 1992/93. Andy Cole celebrates completing his hat-trick in the 89th minute in front of a 10,174 (£64,826) crowd on 25 August. City won 5-1 to progress into the second round of the League Cup 5-2 on aggregate.

Right: Bristol City *v.* Charlton Athletic, 1992/93. In front of 9,286 fans, who paid receipts of £43,299.50, City's Russell Osman (right) keeps his eye on the ball in an aerial tussle with Carl Leaburn. The match, played on 10 October, was a 2-1 home success.

Bristol City *v*. Charlton Athletic, 1992/93. Brian Mitchell (centre) clears City's lines during the 2-1 win on 10 October. The other City players in the picture are Leroy Rosenior (left) and (right) Andy Cole.

Bristol City *v*. Charlton Athletic, 1993/93. Further action from this game shows City's Jacki Dziekanowski holding off a challenge.

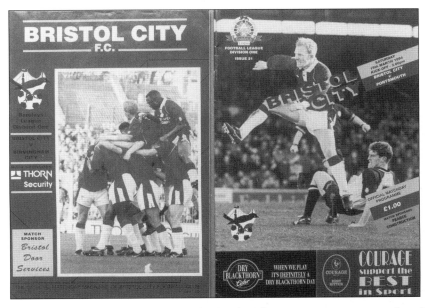

Bristol City programme 1992/93 and 1993/94. *Left:* This programme was produced for the meeting with Birmingham City on 7 November, when goals from Andy Cole, Leroy Rosenior and Gary Shelton brought a 3-0 success in front of an 10,019 (£48,551.00) crowd. *Right:* A Wayne Allison goal brought City a single goal win over Portsmouth, watched by 6,352 (£29,476.50) spectators, on 19 March.

Bristol City *v.* Charlton Athletic, 1993/94. The fans entering the Open End for this game played on 18 September, when a 7,484 crowd (£36,271) witnessed a goal-less draw. This portion of the ground was last used by standing spectators almost six months later on 5 March, when a goal-less draw was played out with Derby County in front of 8,723 fans who generated receipts of £44,653.

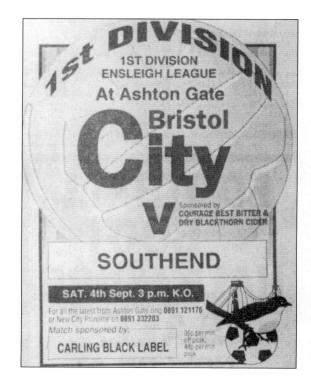

Bristol City *v*. Southend United, 1993/94. Don't be fooled by this match advertisement, which appeared in the *Bristol Evening Post*. City haven't regained former top-flight glory, in fact their status is now akin to the late 1890s, when as a Southern League club they operated in the second tier of English football. The formation of the Premier League in 1992 reduced the status of the Football League, even though the loss of so many clubs meant City became a First Division club once more. Receipts of £35,899.50 were realised from the 7,392 crowd who saw City lose 2-1.

Scandinavian Supporters Club, 1993/94. Some members of the Scandinavian Supporters meet with the City during Christmas. From left to right: Brian Tinnion, Martin Scott, Tyefil Nordhus, Andrew Jefferson, Goran Pendersen, Alexander Boe, Liam Robinson. The origins of this Supporters Club, formed by Goran Penderson, was due to City's brief moment of fame following their 1989/90 FA Cup success over Chelsea.

Liverpool *v*. Bristol City, 1993/94. Brian Tinnion (left) fires in the goal that brings City their famous FA Cup replay success at in front of a 36,720 Anfield crowd (£337,909.50) on 25 January.

The Park (Open) End 1993/94. A final view of the Open End after City's final game of the season which saw Peterborough beaten 4-1 in front of a 7,790 crowd, paying receipts of £33,522.50, on 8 May. As can be seen, work has just commenced on what was to be known as the Atyeo Stand.

The Park End, 1994/95. View from the Atyeo Stand on City's Open Day shows that work is still in progress on the new structure. Strangely, the part that can be seen here, designated as Block A, was completed without a roof.

Bristol City *v.* Sunderland, 1994/95. The new season opened with this goal-less draw against old rivals Sunderland. Unfortunately for the 11,127 crowd, who paid receipts of £81,203.50, the new stand wasn't yet ready for use, as this photograph of Wayne Allison's header hitting the outside of the net shows.

Bristol City *v.* Notts County, 1994/95. The newly opened Atyeo Stand provides the backdrop as Junior Bent makes progress down the right wing in City's 2-1 win in front of a 6,670 (£35,205.50) crowd on 10 September.

City programme 1994/95 and 1995/96. *Left:* The cover of this issue for the Sunderland game on 13 August shows young fans having fun on City's open day. *Right:* This issue for the game against Swansea City, which was won 1-0 in front of a 6,845 crowd (£40,365.50) on 26 December has a fine action picture of Brian Tinnion on the cover.

Bristol City *v.* Huddersfield Town, 1994/95. Action from City's 4-3 success in the quarter-finals of the Women's FA Cup on 12 February. A crowd of some 600 on the DRG ground at Shortwood saw substitute Louise Drury grab City's injury time winner.

Bristol City *v.* Luton Town, 1994/95. City's Brian Tinnion powers past Luton's Julian James during a thrilling 2-2 draw. Unfortunately, it proved not to be Tinnion's day as, in front of a 7,939 (£43,295.00) crowd on 25 February, he had his 43rd minute penalty saved by Juergen Sommer.

Now you see them, now you don't. The tobacco bond warehouses that had for so long been part of the Ashton Gate scene are shown being blown up at 9.30am on Sunday, 26 February 1995.

Junior Reds, 1994/95. The Junior Reds in action opposite the Ashton Gate ground in Greville Smythe Park on 18 March.

Bristol City *v*. Liverpool, 1994/95. Unfortunately, City proved no match for Liverpool in the Women's FA Cup semi-final played on Mangotsfield United's Cossam Street ground. They lost 5-0 in front of a 1,800 crowd on 19 March.

Bristol City Reserves *v*. Chelsea Reserves, 1994/95. A crowd of just 248 were at the Hand Stadium, Clevedon, on 6 May for this Football Combination game. City used the ground for many of their reserves games this season because of concerns over the Ashton Gate pitch. This photograph shows City's coach, Clive Whitehead, a member of City's promotion winning side of 1975/76, taking a corner.

Above: The 99th Gloucestershire Senior Professional Cup Final 1996/97. Played at Ashton Gate in front of a 4,932 crowd, the picture shows the City players with the Cup, which they won for the 54th time thanks to Shaun Goater's late goal. Unfortunately, this proved to be the end of a competition, which had started in 1887 when it was won by the Clifton Association club. The City and Rovers now field their reserve sides against the likes of Cinderford, Cirencester, Forest Green and Mangotsfield in the Gloucestershire Challenge Cup, a competition which formerly had been for clubs in the north of the county.

Left: Bristol City *v.* Burnley, 1996/97. City's Shaun Goater (centre), makes sure that no one crowds his space during the 2-1 home success of 11 January, which generated £52,338.90 receipts from a crowd of 10,013.

Bristol City programmes, 1996/97 and 1997/98. *Left:* After City had started the season with an elongated style of programme it was back to normal by the time Bournemouth won this game 1-0, in front of a 10,434 (£55,326.40) crowd on 25 January. *Right:* Success this time for City as, in front of 9,043 fans on 16 August, Blackpool are beaten 2-0.

Left: Buster Footman was City's popular physiotherapist for ten years until stepping down at the end of the 1998/99 season, when he took on the part-time role of kit-man. A former Royal Marine Commando, Buster is a legend at Ashton Gate as no matter how bitterly cold the weather he spurns any warm clothing and always appears on match days wearing his flimsy short-sleeved shirt. Renowned for his many daredevil stunts for charity, he was unfortunate in February 2000 when his attempt to climb Mount Kilimanjaro ended just short of the summit. *Right: Green 'Un*, 1997/98. The start of the season on 9 August brought about the welcome return of Bristol's popular sports paper after an absence of eighteen years. City managed a 1-1 draw at Grimsby, despite losing their new £400,000 striker Steve Torpey with a horrific head injury.

Bristol City's FA Cup final memorabilia. *Left:* Coloured serviette souvenir, belonging to Mark Britton, of City's one and only FA Cup final appearance. *Right:* City chairman Scott Davidson is shown in January 1999 with memorabilia of that great day 90 years before. The framed blue shirt and the runners-up medal attached to the bottom of the garment belonged to Frederick Staniforth, City's centre-forward in the 1-0 defeat by Manchester United at the Crystal Palace on 26 April 1909. The Pathe disc was produced to go with a film of the final, which was originally shown at both the Princes and the Empire Theatres during the week following the game. Found again in a London junk shop almost 26 years later, it was purchased for just 9d and returned to Bristol for showing at the Town Hall, Bedminster in February 1935. (The purchase of the Pathe disc by the City Chairman raised hopes of tracking down the film, which David Woods had traced as being given up to the safekeeping of the Bristol City Council at the outbreak of the Second World War. Scott Davidson's help was enlisted to open some doors, but unfortunately, after an extensive search, the film was not discovered in the Council archives. It is likely that it was destroyed in 1941 when the museum, where the film had probably been stored, was bombed.)

Oppposite below:

Left: Bristol City programme, 1998/99. A large magazine style was in vogue for this season only as is illustrated by this issue for the Bradford City game on 20 March, which was lost 3-2 in front of a 10,870 crowd. Unfortunately, the opportunity to produce something special with the extra space on offer was lost as the font size was much increased.

Right: Bristol City programme, 1999/2000. The issue for the game versus AFC Bournemouth, which was won 3-1, in front of 11,315 on 14 August, is typical of the style of this season's productions.

Bristol City *v*. Norwich City, 1998/99. In front of a 10,856 crowd, Lorenzo Pinamonte marks his debut on 9 May with the only goal of the game in the 39th minute to enable City to close down their disastrous campaign with a rare victory.

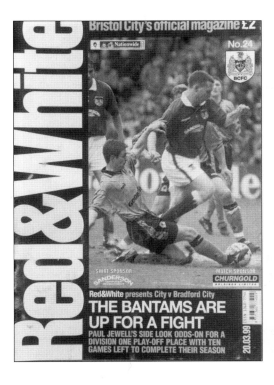

Left: *Green 'Un* 1999/2000. The front page of the *Green 'Un* for 19 February shows action from City's 2-2 home draw with Notts County, which was watched by a 10,029 crowd.

Below: Bristol City programme, 2000/01 and 2001/02. *Left:* The programme had a catchy name, but it was a pity about the thick cardboard-type paper used for the cover, which was reminiscent of 1986/87. The 10,637 crowd present for the game were not particularly concerned about that though, as they saw Cambridge beaten 6-2. *Right:* The cover picture was more varied this season, although the use of overthick paper remained. Stoke City, on their way to a successful place in the play-offs, drew 2-2 in front of an 11,227 crowd on 20 April.

Cinderford Town *v*. Bristol City Reserves, 2001/02. Pre-season action from City's 1-0 defeat in the delayed 2000/01 Gloucestershire Senior Challenge Cup Final played at Cinderford on 31 July in front of a gathering of just 322 spectators.

Northampton Town *v*. Bristol City, 2001/02. Tony Thorpe nets his third goal in the 28th minute as City start the season in great form with a 3-0 success, in front of a 5,528 crowd at the Sixfields Stadium on 11 August.

A concise illustrated history of Bristol City FC by Paul Thatcher

AFTER THE EXCITEMENT OF DEFEATING MIGHTY LEEDS IN THE '74 FA CUP, FIFTH SPOT THE FOLLOWING SEASON REPRESENTED CITY'S BEST FINISH UNDER ALAN DICKS. ALL OF THIS MEANT CITY WOULD BEGIN THE 75/76 CAMPAIGN IN A QUIETLY CONFIDENT MOOD

CITY JOSTLED WITH SUNDERLAND & WBA FOR TOP SPOT FOR MOST OF THE SEASON, BUT WITH GARY COLLIER, GEOFF MERRICK, GERRY GOW & WHAT SEEMED LIKE THE ENTIRE SQUAD PERFORMING AT THE PEAK OF THEIR POWERS, CITY ENTERED THE FINAL FURLONG JUST IN FRONT.

THE FINAL TEN GAMES PROVED TO BE A NERVY PERIOD, BUT NOT EVEN A FLU EPIDEMIC COULD STOP CITY. GERRY SWEENEY'S WINNER AT THE HAWTHORNS EDGED CITY CLOSER TO PROMOTION & WHEN OVER 27,000 SAW CLIVE WHITEHEAD RAM THE WINNER VERSUS POMPEY THE REDS MADE IT PAST THE POST IN 2ND PLACE & RETURNED TO THE 1ST DIVISION FOR THE FIRST TIME IN 65 ROLLER COASTER YEARS!!!!!

THE REDS BEGAN WITH TWO WINS, BUT TWO DEFEATS FOLLOWED, MEANING CITY WERE IN SEVENTH SPOT. PAUL CHEESLEY'S GOAL AGAINST ROVERS IN A 1-1 DRAW WAS HIS FIRST OF ELEVEN IN A NINE GAME SPELL & HIS PARTNERSHIP WITH TOM RITCHIE HAD HELPED CITY TO TOP SPOT BY THE END OF OCTOBER!!

thatch '00

Paul Thatcher's cartoons were a feature of City's programme throughout the 1999/2000 season. This example of his work, which depicts the 1975/76 promotion campaign, comes from the issue for the Preston North End game, which was lost 2-0 in front of an 11,160 crowd on 6 May.

Acknowledgements

The photographs in this book have come from many sources, including the Bristol City programme, *Western Daily Press*, *Bristol Evening Post*, *Football Monthly*, *League Football*, and *Soccer Star* as well as those taken by David Woods himself and other fans Kevin Brake, Mark Britton, Gerry Pearce and Edward Woods. The professional photographers whose work is displayed here include Owen Barnes, John Cottle, Malcolm Croft, Terry Dite, J.P. Fluck, Jack Garland, Peter Haynes, Ralph Hudd, Richard Hudd, David Katz, John Kelland, Richard Mitchell and Nigel Ollis.